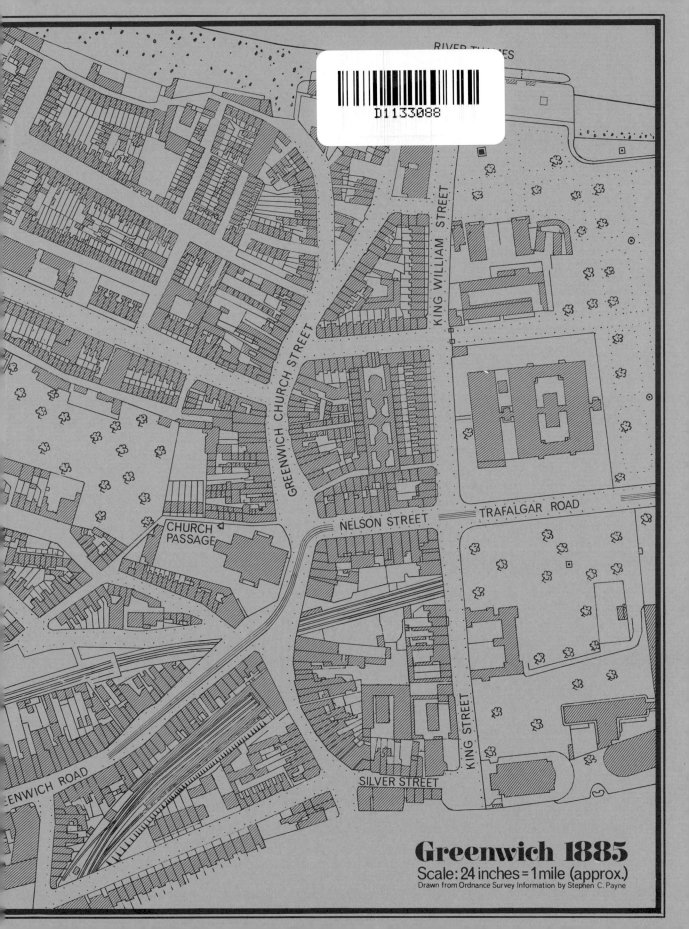

Greenwich 1885

Scale: 24 inches = 1 mile (approx.)
Drawn from Ordnance Survey Information by Stephen C. Payne

To Brownie and Jack
a little bit of old England
With Love
Sheila and David
October 1981

Grandfather's Greenwich

Shine yer boots Sir? Mr Spurgeon anticipates Hitchcock by half a century and appears in his own photograph. Greenwich, August Bank Holiday Monday 1884.

Grandfather's Greenwich

*By
Alan Glencross
with Photographs
from the Spurgeon Collection*

CONWAY MARITIME PRESS
1972

Thamesmead Histories
Volume IV

First Published 1972
© Conway Maritime Press Ltd.,
7 Nelson road, Greenwich, London, S.E.10
ISBN 0 85177 061 4

Typography
and Design/**Jon Blackmore**
Cartography/**Stephen C Payne**
Set in 11/13 pt Journal by PJB Typesetting
and Printed in Great Britain by Latimer Trend Ltd.,
Whitstable, Kent

Contents

INTRODUCTION *by Alan Glencross*   *Page* 7

KNIFEBOARD BUS *Going to Greenwich — London Bridge station*
approach. 1887.   10

APPLES, MATCHES, SANDWICHES *Borough High Street 1887*   11

HANSOM CAB *Outside Greenwich Station 1885*   12

CHAIRS TO MEND! *Greenwich Road 1885*   13

STOP THIEF! *Blackheath Road Police Station 1885*   14

A FAIR COP *Blackheath Road Police Station 1885*   14

THE CUP THAT CHEERS *Greenwich Church Street 1885*   15

CATS' MEAT! *King Street 1885*   16

NICE TOYS FOR GIRLS AND BOYS! *King William Street 1884*   17

ANY FRESH SALARY? *King Street 1885*   18

POSTMAN *King Street 1885*   19

RABBITS *Greenwich 1885*   20

FIRE! FIRE! *Grove Street fire station 1885*   21

MILK HO! *King William Street 1885*   22

MUFFINS AND CRUMPETS *Greenwich 1885*   23

OLD CLO! *Greenwich 1885*   24

SHINE SIR? *London Bridge Station Approach 1887*   25

UNDER THE YOKE *King Street 1884*   26

SHERBERT — HA'PENNY A GLASS *King Street August Bank*
Holiday Monday 1884   27

MUSIC HATH CHARMS *King Street August Monday 1884* 28
A MAN OF PUSH *King William Street 1885* 29
THE THREEPENNY BUMPER *Trafalgar Road 1885* 30
SWEE—EE—P! *King Street 1884* 31
GINGER CAKES *King Street 1884* 32
MEND YER WINDERS! *King Street 1885* 33
REMEMBER THE SWEEPER! *King William Street 1885* 34
FINE SHRIMPS! *King Street August Monday 1884* 35
ALL A—GROWN AND A—BLOWIN! *London Street 1885* 36
COALS! COALS! *Ravensbourne Street 1885* 37
SHINE YER BOOTS SIR? *Roan Street August Monday 1884* 38
FRESH 'ERBS! *London Street 1885* 39
KENTISH HAY *Greenwich Road 1885* 40
PIE—PER! *King William Street 1885* 41
PITY THE POOR BLIND *Silver Street August Monday 1884* 42
HOKEY POKEY *London Street August Monday 1884* 43
OVERTURE *King Street 1884* 44
FIRE DRILL *Grove Street Fire Station 1885* 46
GROWLERS *South Eastern Railway 1885* 47
THE CHAMPION *Church Passage August Monday 1884* 48
FISH ALL ALIVE *King Street 1884* 49
ETHIOPIAN SERENADERS *King Street 1884* 50
CROCKS! CROCKS! *King Street 1884* 51
TRY YOUR WEIGHT! *King Street August Monday 1884* 52
FINALE *King Street 1884* 53
HEAD GUARD *South Eastern Railway 1885* 54
INTERVAL *King Street 1884* 55
OLD AND NEW BUSES *London Bridge Approach 1887* 56
ALL IN THE DAYS WORK *Blackheath Road Police Station 1885* 57
KNIVES AND SCISSORS TO GRIND! *London Street August Monday 1885* 58
ANY LIGHTS SIR? *King Street 1884* 59/60 & 61
PLATFORM PORTERS *South Eastern Railway 1885* 62
POLICE AMBULANCE *Blackheath Road Police Station 1885* 63

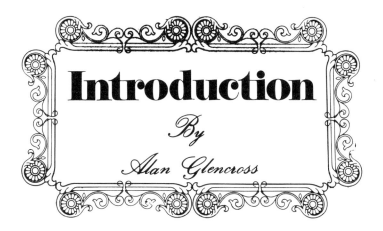

Introduction

By
Alan Glencross

The photographs in this book were taken between 1884 and 1887, mainly in Greenwich, to illustrate a lantern lecture on working class life in the area. Between them they constitute a unique, if somewhat selective, pictorial record of the streets of Greenwich, and the characters who thronged them, almost ninety years ago. The record is selective because it was commissioned by a Baptist minister for showing to respectable (and presumably middle class) audiences; consequently nothing is portrayed which in any way suggests intemperance, vice or ribaldry, for that would have shocked and antagonized the people to whom it was addressed. The evidence of poverty, squalor, exploitation and lack of hygiene which some of the pictures present, and which may shock us today, were then accepted as natural.

This collection of pictures may be said to be the work of three men: the Rev Charles Spurgeon, who commissioned the photographs, the unidentified professional photographer who took them (possibly Mr R Sims of King Street, Greenwich) and Mr O J Morris, a transport historian and photographer, who seventy years later presented the original proof photographs to Greenwich Libraries.

Spurgeon was born in 1856, the twin son of the Rev Charles Haddon Spurgeon (of the Metropolitan Tabernacle). Originally intended for a commercial career, he became a lay preacher. After training at the Spurgeon

College he entered the Baptist ministry, and was minister of South Street Baptist Church, Greenwich from 1879 to 1903. He died in 1926. Spurgeon was a pioneer, not in using the lantern lecture as a means of propaganda or even in having his slides made from photographs, but in commissioning for his purpose a special set of authentic representations of the everyday life of the day. It has been claimed that these photographs constitute the first photo-documentary: they are certainly among the earliest.

Such an enterprise had only recently become a practical possibility with two developments in photographic technique which took place in the early 1880's. The introduction of the dry-plate process had made possible the use of previously-prepared plates and their subsequent processing in the darkroom, enabling the photographer to dispense with the mobile darkroom which had hitherto been an essential encumbrance to the practice of outdoor photography, while improved emulsions had drastically reduced exposure times to the point where the illusion of spontaneity could be achieved.

It *is* an illusion: Spurgeon's photographs seem to be instantaneous and his subjects stand naturally with no evidence of strain, but each picture was carefully composed and the poses must have been held for at least a second. An occasional background blur where a bystander has moved or a vehicle has passed during the exposure give the game away. Some of the extras make more than one appearance and indeed Mr Spurgeon himself anticipated Alfred Hitchcock by half a century and played a number of walk-on parts in his own production. He can be seen having his patent leather boots polished in no. 30, leaning negligently on the hokey-pokey cart in no. 35, and travelling by train in no. 52.

The original photographs were half-plate. The negatives and the slides have been lost but the proof prints, made by the albumen process, survive, although many of them are badly faded. These prints passed from Mr Spurgeon to his son-in-law, the Rev Alfred Cunningham Burley, and from him to Mr O J Morris. In 1955 Mr Morris presented them to Greenwich Libraries, who sponsored his production of a set of copies. It was these copies which Mr Morris used in his book *Grandfather's London* (Putnam, 1956 o.p.), and they have also been used in preparing this book.

The titles of the photographs and the order in which they are presented were determined by Mr Spurgeon. They throw some light on the street cries common at the time and may also offer some hints to the nature of the commentary with which he accompanied their presentation on his magic lantern.

1. KNIFEBOARD BUS.

London Bridge Station Approach, 1887.

A 26-seater 'bus operated by the London General Omnibus Co., a development of a prize-winning design of the 1850's. The improvement in design consisted principally of the replacement of bracket steps to the roof by the ladders shewn here. Notice the lack of uniforms and the depot code and duty letter (C-H), a forerunner of modern practice. 'Buses on each of the ten or so routes operating from London Bridge Station had different coloured liveries; this one was yellow.

2. APPLES, MATCHES, SANDWICHES.

Borough High Street, 1887.

The apples and matches are being peddled by the two women in the gutter, the *Sandwiches* are carried by the sandwich-board men beyond. The viewpoint is from the east side of Borough High Street, under the railway bridge, and looking towards London Bridge.

3. HANSOM CAB.

Outside Greenwich Station, 1885.

The Hansom cab was the fastest and most elegant public conveyance on the road. It was invented in 1836 by John Chapman and superseded an earlier, clumsier two-wheel cab invented by Joseph Aloysius Hansom. Thomas Tilling was the most esteemed of London's public carriers. Besides his 'bus and cab interests he provided horses (often matched greys, for which his stud was famous) to, among others, the Metropolitan Board of Works, the Metropolitan Fire Brigade, Queen Victoria's Golden Jubilee procession and the Lord Mayor's Show.

4. CHAIRS TO MEND!

Greenwich Road, 1885

The corner of Greenwich Road, now Greenwich High Road, and Prince of Orange Lane. The lane, a narrow cul-de-sac, is still paved with setts, while the shop on the corner (also seen in no. 32) is still a baker's.

14

5/6. STOP, THIEF! A FAIR COP.

Blackheath Road Police Station, 1885.

The garden behind the Section House, with villas (now demolished) on the east side of Catherine Grove in the background. The Greenwich Magistrate's Court, Juvenile Court and Maurice Drummond House, now occupy this site.

7. THE CUP THAT CHEERS.

Greenwich Church Street, 1885.

Outside St. Alphege's Church, opposite the end of Nelson Street, now Nelson Road. The photograph was taken about 8 a.m. The unsold fragment of current cake, the drying teaclothes and the bucket overflowing with discarded cake wrappings all suggest that the morning rush was already nearly over.

8. CATS' MEAT!

King Street, 1885.

What is now King William Walk was then King Street from the Park gates to Nelson Road and King William Street from there to the Pier. This photograph was taken on the east side of the street, which caught the afternoon sun and was a favourite haunt of pedlars. This one dealt in squares of horsemeat, impaled on a skewer and sold at a penny a dozen. The state of his boots and the cart wheels indicate the condition of the roads at that time.

9. NICE TOYS
FOR GIRLS AND BOYS!

King William Street, 1884.

The west side of the street, with the railings of the Royal Naval College in the background. Windmills, paper sunshades, flags and songsheets on sale from a hired barrow.

11. POSTMAN.

King Street, 1885.

The house, the only one on the east side of the street, and next to St. Mary's Church, belonged to Dr Armstrong. It has since been demolished.

10. ANY FRESH 'SALARY'?

King Street, 1885.

The east side of the street.

19

20

12. RABBITS.

Greenwich, 1885.

This location has not been traced. Eight rabbits carried into Greenwich, probably from rural Eltham, Lee or Catford, and hawked round the streets, seven of them still unsold. The girdle of sacking was intended to keep the blood off the vendor's coat.

13. FIRE! FIRE!

Grove Street Fire Station, 1885.

The yard behind the station in Grove Street, now Lindsell Street. The station has been rebuilt, and now fronts Blissett Street. The photograph shows a Merryweather steam water-pump (made in Greenwich) with its crew. The turncock, standing on the left, would in fact have gone straight to the scene of the fire. The stoker-fireman, at the rear, was expected to build up a full head of steam (100 lbs p.s.i.) *en route.* The fireman standing on the driver's right was the 'Hi! Hi!' man, who shouted to clear the way. Warning bells had not yet been introduced.

15. MUFFINS AND CRUMPETS.

Greenwich, 1885.

This location has not been traced.

14. MILK HO!

King William Street, 1885.

Outside the Royal Naval College. The master milkman, presumably J Dymond, proprietor of the Devonshire Dairy, wears the traditional uniform of dark blue monkey jacket and long apron.

24

16. OLD CLO!

Greenwich, 1885.

This location has not been traced. The man was collecting, not selling, old clothes, and paying for his acquisitions in coin or in kind.

17. SHINE SIR?

London Bridge Station Approach 1887.

The railway bridge is still there, but a later bridge has been built on the near side. The boy was a member of the Shoeblack Brigade, founded by the 7th Earl of Shaftesbury, and was licensed to work a pitch. In theory his takings were shared: one-third to the boy in cash, one-third into his Savings Bank account and one-third to the Brigade. In fact, 'fiddling' was rife.

18. UNDER THE YOKE.

King Street, 1884.

Outside 13 King William Walk. The shop front has since been removed. The weight when full of the two four-gallon cans which the milkman carried on his yoke was about 80 lbs.

19. SHERBERT HA'PENNY A GLASS.

King Street, August Monday, 1884.

By the Park gates, opposite the end of Silver Street (now Nevada Street). It was the photographer, and not the barefoot boy, who attracted attention; ragged clothes like this were commonplace.

20. MUSIC HATH CHARMS.

King Street, August Monday, 1884.

21. A MAN OF PUSH.

King William Street, 1885.

The Royal Naval College in the background. An employee of the master milkman of no. 14, this man had a load of about 4 cwt to push.

23. SWEE-EE-P!
King Street, 1884.

22.
THE THREEPENNY BUMPER.
Trafalgar Road, 1885.

The Greenwich tram terminus near Christ Church. A two-mule, *knife-board* car with 40 seats, operated by the London Tramway Co., this tram had a blue livery. Cars running from this terminus to Blackfriars were painted red.

30

25. MEND YER WINDERS!

King Street, 1885.

The side goods entrance to 22/23 Nelson Street, now built over.

24. GINGER CAKES.

King Street, 1884.

The west side of the street, looking towards Trafalgar Road. Possibly a Saturday afternoon.

34

26.
REMEMBER THE SWEEPER!

King William Street, 1885.

At the corner of Clarence Street (now College Approach). In wet weather the streets could only be crossed in comfort at these paved crossings. This one has disappeared, but many others can still be seen in the neighbourhood.

27. FINE SHRIMPS!

King Street, August Monday, 1884.

Outside the Park gates with the wall of St. Mary's Church behind. The poster advertises the restaurant in the Park Pavilion.

28. ALL
A-GROWIN' AND A-BLOWIN'.

London Street, 1885.

The houses are now 199-213 Greenwich High Road.

29. COALS! COALS!

Ravensbourne Street, 1885.

The northern end of what is now Norman Road, near the junction with Pearson Street (now Haddo Street). This terrace has since been demolished.

31. FRESH 'ERBS.

London Street, 1885.

The houses are those seen in no. 28. Herbsellers like this girl regularly walked into Greenwich from country districts as far afield as Bexleyheath.

30. SHINE YER BOOTS, SIR?

Roan Street, August Monday, 1884.

The shop is probably 1, Brunswick Terrace, Straightsmouth (now 2 Churchfield and still standing), at the junction with Roan Street. It was then occupied by Thomas Welman, Marine Store Dealer. The boy was an unlicensed *independent*, not allowed to pitch, and liable to be moved on by the police.

33. PIE-PER!

King William Street, 1885.

The west side of the street, near the Pier, about 7.30 a.m.

32. KENTISH HAY

Greenwich Road, 1885.

Opposite the end of South Street, with **Prince of Orange Lane** in the background. The fountain (provided by the Metropolitan Drinking Fountain and Cattle Trough Association and supplying Thames water) has been replaced by a public lavatory. The Association still operates, from an office in Lewisham High Street.

41

42

34. PITY THE POOR BLIND.

Silver Street, August Monday, 1884.

Crowder's Music Hall became the *Parthenon* in 1885 and was owned by the licensee of the *Rose and Crown* next door. Subsequently *Barnard's* and the *Hippodrome,* and in turn a music hall, a cinema and a furniture warehouse, it is now the Greenwich Theatre.

35. HOKEY-POKEY.

London Street, August Monday, 1884.

The parapet of the railway bridge at the foot of Stockwell Street. *Hokey-pokey* may seem an archaism to us, but Mr Spurgeon may have chosen this title to demonstrate how up-to-date he was. Its earliest use to describe cheap ice-cream is recorded in Partridge's *Dictionary of slang* as *circa 1884.*

44

36. OVERTURE.

King Street, 1884.

Outside 8 and 9 King William Walk.

46

37. FIRE DRILL.

Grove Street Fire Station, 1885.

A staged display by the Metropolitan Fire Brigade. The crew are the same as in no. 13, with the addition of the Salvage Man. The pump is manually operated.

38. GROWLERS.

South Eastern Railway, 1885.

This is probably Maze Hill Station. It might possibly be Westcombe Park, but the cabbing rights there were held by Clark of Blackheath, whereas Tilling's cabs plied from Maze Hill as from Greenwich. These Tilling four-wheelers were officially *Clarences* but colloquially *Growlers*.

48

39. THE CHAMPION.

Church Passage, August Monday, 1884.

What is now St. Alphege's Passage, looking towards Greenwich Church Street. The shop is no longer there but the entry posts of the end of the lane remain. W Thompson stands at his shop door with the charcoal-heated hot-pot he carried on his rounds. It was this picture which enabled Morris to date the Bank Holiday photographs: the revival of 'Black-eyed See-usan', advertised on the playbill in the window, opened at the Alhambra on the Saturday before August Monday, 1884.

40. FISH ALL ALIVE.

King Street, 1885.

Outside 8 and 9 King William Walk, which are little changed.

41. ETHIOPIAN SERENADERS.

King Street, 1884.

The east side of the street.

42. CROCKS! CROCKS!

King Street, 1884.

10a to 10d King William Walk now occupy the site of the London and Naval Hotel, late Swigg's.

44. FINALE.

King Street, 1884.

The sequel to No 36.

43. TRY YOUR WEIGHT!

King Street, August Monday, 1884.

Outside the Park gates, with St. Mary's Church (demolished 1935) in the background. The spring balance and try-your-strength machine can also be seen in no. 19.

45. HEAD GUARD.

South Eastern Railway, 1885.

    This is probably Maze Hill Station. The engine is a *Gunboat* 0-4-4 tank, one of nine built at Ashford in 1877-78; it was liveried green. The passenger brake van, which probably dated from the 1850's, was purple-brown and salmon-pink. Passenger trains then carried two guards; the Head Guard, who travelled immediately behind the engine in the compartment with the *birdcage* lookout on the roof, is here seen giving the 'right, forward' signal to his subordinate at the rear of the train.

46. INTERVAL.

King Street, 1884.

Outside the King's Arms (since rebuilt) in King William Walk. Street pianos were an English invention, but their operation became an Italian monopoly.

47. OLD AND NEW 'BUSES.

London Bridge Station Approach, 1887.

The *knifeboard* bus on the left ran to Swiss Cottage, and was liveried dark green. The *garden-seat* 'bus, also dark green, ran to Finsbury Park. This was the first London General route to be equipped with these 'buses, which had been introduced by the London Road Car Co. in 1881. They had a platform, proper stairs, cross seats — and a foot-brake! Knifeboard 'buses had no brakes at all.

48. ALL IN THE DAYS WORK.

Blackheath Road Police Station, 1885.

49. KNIVES
AND SCISSORS TO GRIND!

London Street, August Monday, 1885.

At the bottom of Stockwell Street, near the hokey-pokey cart seen in no. 35. Besides knife-grinding and tinkering (he is seen cutting a kettle bottom from a sheet of tinplate) this man seems also to have dealt in old umbrellas.

50/51. ANY LIGHTS, SIR.

King Street, 1884.

No. 50 has been widely reproduced, and is perhaps the best known photograph in this collection. The boy, with his jaunty stance and determined expression, presents to us a romanticised picture of Victorian street life; one feels that by perseverance and industry and self-help he would surely rise in the world, and that he is already taking the first step out of the gutter. Seen full-face, in no. 51, he is less appealing. His expression is sullen and his face looks bruised and battered. This may well have been the case; he was probably one of a gang employed by a factor, lodged under vile conditions and often ill-treated by their employer. The *Alpine Vesuvians* he sold were long-headed, slow-burning fusee matches which would burn in any wind. They cost 1d. for a box of 20.

52. PLATFORM PORTERS.

South Eastern Railway, 1885.

Presumably the same station as no. 45. The coach was then one of the latest type of suburban third class coaches, and was painted maroon, a livery which had been recently introduced. It had a continuous footboard, wooden seats with no upholstery and oil lighting.

53. POLICE AMBULANCE.

Blackheath Road Police Station, 1885.

Ambulances of this type were kept at all Metropolitan Police Stations until the 1930's.

The Spurgeon photographs are in the collection of the Greenwich Libraries Local History Centre, 'Woodlands', Mycenae Road, S.E.3. They, and material from the catalogue of the Greenwich Libraries Exhibition, 'Mr Spurgeon's Greenwich' (1969), are reproduced by kind permission of the Recreational Services Committee of the London Borough of Greenwich.